LEBRON JAMES

KING OF THE COURT

JOHN EMERSON

LEBRON JAMES
Copyright © 2016 by John Emerson

CONTENTS

Introduction

"Akron, Ohio, is my home. It will always be remembered. Akron, Ohio Is my life." – LeBron James

CROWDS OF EAGER CLEVELAND FANS waited patiently for the King to step on stage. Almost overnight, the atmosphere of Cleveland had completely changed. What was once a desolate and desperate town had now received a blessing, and once again the city of Cleveland had reason to celebrate. New life was being breathed into the city, and just like those awaiting a long lost soldier returning from battle, crowds of proud, excited fans were waiting to celebrate a triumphant return.

Describe this situation to any Cleveland Cavalier

fan or NBA enthusiast four years ago, and chances are they wouldn't believe you. This was a complete 180-degree turn of events from what had conspired throughout the last four years. In that time, the NBA landscape had completely shifted - all due to an unprecedented move by one NBA player.

One NBA player, one former hometown hero - and now a former hero turned villain, reviled across all the NBA's landscape. Who knew that just one player could affect millions of lives with six short words that would send shockwaves throughout the entire league. It crushed the hearts of Cleveland fans for thousands of miles across the nation to see their once beloved hometown hero flee to Miami to join the Miami Heat. Throughout the entire world, many people turned their heads to the NBA in utter shock and uproar. Only one player has ever had this kind of monumental effect on the entire league: LeBron James.

LeBron had gone from the hometown hero, destined to save Cleveland from their miserable championship drought, to being one of the most hated players throughout the NBA.

But now, just four years after his fateful "decision" to join the Miami Heat, LeBron had returned to Cleveland. It was the end of the 2014 NBA season, and there was a special Welcome Home rally being held for the prodigal son's return.

"Ladies and gentlemen, please welcome home the James family," the announcer spoke as crowds of excited fans began to cheer incessantly.

The fans, the Cavalier owners, and the entire city that had once shunned LeBron now embraced him with open arms. Finally, they had something to look forward to once more - a future where their dreams of bringing sporting glory to Cleveland were now rekindled. He was no longer a villain; he was now a champion – a bona fide "King" after winning two championships with the Miami Heat. Now, he was ready to bring that same glory back to Cleveland.

"I'm not having a press conference or a party," he said at the rally. "After this, it's time to get to work."

LeBron James was now on a different mission. The small kid from Akron had already summited basketball's highest peak, but now it was time to do it once again for the town he owed so much to. Once again, he had shaken the NBA landscape with his return to Cleveland.

Cavalier fans bowed down graciously. Cleveland was now under new rule – their King had officially returned.

CHAPTER ONE

EARLY CHILDHOOD

"I'm going to use all my tools, my God-given ability, and make the best life I can with it."- LeBron James

LEBRON DIDN'T HAVE A NORMAL CHILDHOOD. He was exposed to numerous hardships growing up, and had to live through bouts of the kinds of tough times that most children should never have to experience. Being raised by a single parent, his mother Gloria, he never had a father figure to look up to during his adolescent years. Basketball would fill up this missing piece in LeBron's life, and his role models would be the basketball icons that he so desperately wanted to emulate.

His mother had little LeBron when she was only 16 years old. You could only imagine the trials that Gloria had to endure while raising her child. Being still a teenager, with no job, no money and no husband to help take care of her child, she was completely alone and helpless. How was she going to raise her child to have even a decent life? It almost seemed like an impossible task, and an unnecessary burden. Little did she know that her child would grow up to be one of the greatest athletes of all time, and to be an incredible blessing to her and an inspiration to millions of people around the world.

LeBron Raymone James was born on 30th December 1984 into a shaky and unsure world. His single mother moved from job to job and apartment to apartment, trying her very best to keep her child and herself afloat. LeBron's early childhood experiences were extremely unstable, and in a world so shaken and moving all the time, he struggled to build any roots or grounding in his life. Normally, experiences like these would cause a young child to be resentful towards the world, particularly to the environment he grew up in – but not for LeBron. From these early ages, his love for his hometown of Akron, Ohio had grown and matured as he in turn grew and developed. His entire life, no matter how shaky and unstable, *was* Cleveland, and it was only when basketball came into his life was he able to give back to the city he so loved.

In an effort to impart some stability into LeBron's life, his mother made the difficult but necessary decision to let him stay and move into the home of a local football coach, Frank Walker. Frank had a stable family environment, and Gloria thought that this was the type of upbringing her son deserved. Finally, LeBron could feel the sense of family and warmth in his life, and his love for his foster family and his city only grew from there.

Gloria probably didn't know it at the time, but letting little LeBron stay with Walker was the most pivotal event so far in LeBron's life. It was only when he moved in with Walker that he began to play basketball. The coach introduced LeBron to what would be his calling at the age of nine. Right from the beginning, LeBron was hooked on the beautiful game.

Being raised by a football coach, LeBron also grew familiar with that sport as well. It was evident at an early age that he was naturally gifted with athletic abilities that most could only dream about. Unlike many other NBA players, LeBron isn't just a basketball player; he is first and foremost an athlete. NBA stars like Kobe Bryant may be primarily known for their basketball prowess and skill, and while they do possess athletic ability, they would suffer if they were to join any other team sport. Basketball is simply their game.

This wasn't the case for LeBron. Whatever sport he chose, he excelled at. Whether it was football or basketball, he would completely dominate his opponents with his unbelievable athleticism and tenacity. He was an entirely different type of player, relying on completely unique skill set - making him absolutely deadly to his opponents. We are only lucky that LeBron chose to play basketball professionally, so that we were treated to the rise of a King and his amazing brand of basketball on the court.

This natural ability was evident at an early age, as LeBron and his close friends earned time in both local and national spotlights as up-and-coming basketball talents. LeBron and his friends Sian

Cotton, Dru Joyce III and Willie McGee were dubbed "The Fab Four" as they played in the Amateur Athletic Union (AAU) for the Northeast Ohio Shooting Stars.

Even at an early age, LeBron had a flair for the dramatic. In a move that caused massive controversy and debate, LeBron and his friends chose to attend St. Vincent-St. Mary High School together – a predominantly white, private Catholic school. LeBron had already stood out from an early age due to his natural talents, but now he was going to stand out even more when he and his three black friends stepped into uncharted territory at their chosen high school.

LeBron didn't care for the attention stemming from the controversy of four black kids infiltrating a nearly all-white Catholic school, however. Instead, he wanted to put St. Vincent-St. Mary High School's basketball team on the map - and make a name for himself as one of the greatest high school basketball players to ever play the game at the same time. He would become known as so good that college and even NBA scouts would line up for the chance to woo LeBron to join their own teams. Or at least that was his plan. Nobody expected this of him just yet, what with his difficult upbringing. However, his early childhood experiences would drive him to do whatever it took to escape the trenches of abject poverty.

Indeed, basketball was his ticket to a better life. With all the God-given tools he possessed, he was determined to carve out the best life he could for himself and his family.

CHAPTER TWO

HIGH SCHOOL BASKETBALL

"Dream as if you'll live forever, live as if you'll die today." – LeBron James

EARLY ON, LEBRON JAMES SHOWED GLIMPSES OF WHAT WOULD BE HIS FUTURE NICKNAME the moment he stepped onto his first competitive basketball court. High school was the first arena to showcase his brilliance. From the very beginning, he showed huge potential as a freshman for St. Vincent-St. Mary High School, and the raw ore for what would become the brilliant steel of his superstardom was starting to show signs of life within him.

Despite all the controversy surrounding four black teenagers attending a predominantly white and Christian high school, LeBron relished in the limelight. All the attention he had garnered from the controversy had turned into that of spectacle, as scouts and fans from all over the state had begun to hear the growing legend of LeBron James. A 6-foot-7-inch tall small forward with the agility of a point guard, the strength of a center and the overall basketball smarts of a coach, LeBron honestly seemed to have it all. He had the make-up of what was deemed the perfect basketball athlete – and many people knew that athletes like LeBron only came around once in a lifetime.

Comparisons to Magic Johnson and other NBA greats began to spring up as well, as fans simply could not hold back their excitement when witnessing a legend being born before their very eyes.

His first year in high school, LeBron averaged 21 points and 6 rebounds, helping his team to an undefeated season of 27-0 and clinching the Division III State Title in the process. His sophomore year only saw these statistics improve, where his points per game would shoot up to 25.2, and his rebounds to

7.2 per game. By the end of his sophomore year, his fame and popularity had grown to incredible proportions; not only would his name echo in his high school hallways forever, but across the nation's as well –fans would come from all over the state just to watch the LeBron James show. Some of St. Vincent-St. Mary's home games even had to be relocated to the University of Akron's Arena simply to satisfy demand for seats: their own school gyms would get so overcrowded with fans wanting to support LeBron that the school had no choice but to choose to play in other, bigger arenas to accommodate all the fanfare. The King had already begun to make a name for himself; LeBron James was slowly but surely becoming a household name.

Finishing with another stellar season of 26-1 in his sophomore year, LeBron's helped lead his team once again to the title of state champions. He would be named Ohio's Mr. Basketball for his stellar performance.

CHAPTER THREE

THE PRESSURES OF SUCCESS

"There's a lot of pressure put on me. But I don't put a lot of pressure on myself. I feel like if I play my game, it will take care of itself." – LeBron James

HOWEVER, LEBRON'S METEORIC RISE TO STARDOM did not come without its fair share of hardship. LeBron's junior season was one of difficulty and transition for the young superstar. The media attention he had received throughout his first two years of high school basketball had begun to wear on him, and the pressures that came along with being "the best high school basketball player in America right now," according to writer Ryan Jones for SLAM Magazine, also began to take its toll. His game was undoubtedly getting better with each passing year, as his averages across all statistics had gone up once again. However, the mental strain that came along with this had its noticeable effects.

The biggest and most telling of these was St. Vincent-St. Mary's untimely loss in a Division II championship game, ending their back-to-back winning streak. This was devastating not only to the school but particularly to LeBron. He had been the leader of his team throughout his entire young career, and as a leader, he had failed to bring them the glory of another championship. Throw in the massive media storm that LeBron faced on a daily basis, and the results were a weary, tired and overall burnt out LeBron James.

This was The King's first major setback in his playing career, and things only started getting worse from there. Not only did the coveted Division II title elude LeBron and his team, but his team record was beginning to deteriorate as well. What was once an undefeated team in his freshman season had declined to a team with slowly piling losses. Naturally, perfection is always expected when you're within the wingspan of the greatest high school basketball player of that time, and whenever you come up short, critics, fans, analysts and even the players themselves began to doubt just whether or not LeBron deserved to sit on the throne everyone had placed him on. When you're deemed a King, you're expected to rule and dominate by any means necessary – and LeBron was failing to do so. With all the weight of the world on what was in essence just a high school kid's shoulders, it was only a matter of time that LeBron's world would collapse.

Despite his freakishly superhuman abilities on the

court, he had his fair share of problems and obstacles off of it – and his junior season was beginning to show them. This downward spiral led the King to doubt his ability to rule. For the past two years he had been gathering accolade after accolade, garnering massive media attention. Now he was still getting attention, but now it was negative – and he began to loathe it. The accolades would still come as he would be named Ohio's Mr. Basketball once again as well as be given the Gatorade National Player of The Year Award, but for once he did not want any part of the attention he was given.

Conflicted and confused, he didn't know what to do. How many other high school kids had to go through the immense kinds of pressure that come with being an absolute phenom on the floor? He did not know whom to turn to for advice or guidance. It was during this time that LeBron even used marijuana to cope with his on-going struggles.

High School Dropout?

Thoughts of leaving high school early to join the NBA even began to circulate in LeBron's head. No player in NBA history has ever dropped out of high school to pursue a professional career, but if any player had the audacity and potential to actually pull something like that off, it would've been LeBron. He petitioned the NBA to make an adjustment to their draft eligibility rules, thinking that his massive following and popularity would be enough of a boost to help him make history – but to no avail. Just like the championship game, he had failed once again.

The pressures of superstardom wore on LeBron. He simply did not know what to do. He was being scrutinized by tens of thousands on a daily basis, and his recent failures garnered him even more negative attention. With the whole world counting him out, it was up to LeBron himself to pick himself up and make history the only way he knew how – on the basketball court.

Faced with no other option and with nothing but his own steely resolve, LeBron was determined to make his final year in high school one that would be remembered forever. He had already garnered so much negative media attention; all he had to do was turn that attention to showcase something positive instead, and his senior year would be a testament to that as he brought his game to new heights. His natural abilities and athleticism were all still growing and developing, and as a senior in high school his averages would peak across all boards. For the third consecutive year, he was named Ohio's Mr. Basketball once again, with averages of 31.6 points and 9.6 rebounds per game.

This new, awe-inspiring level of play brought LeBron a whole new plethora of fans, and the LeBron James show had become regular sold-out crowd favourite.

At this point, the demand to watch LeBron's basketball prowess was so high that Time Warner Cable began to offer pay-per-view broadcasts of his gmes. For the second year in a row, he was named the Gatorade National Player of The Year Award, scoring a career high of 52 points.

CHAPTER FOUR

EYES ON THE STARS, FEET ON THE GROUND

'I think the reason why I'm the person who I am today is because I went through those tough times when I was younger." – LeBron James

GLORIA JAMES RAN UP TO HER SON and embraced him. The school hallway was crowded with parents and students alike, but Gloria could not contain her excitement any longer.

"That's what I'm talking about! Get a picture of this diploma! I'll hold it up, take a look at this here!" Gloria cried, elated, amidst the crowds of reporters

JOHN EMERSON

surrounding her.

LeBron had just received his high school diploma and successfully graduated alongside the rest of the "Fab Four." The same teenager who only a year ago wanted to drop out of high school had made a complete turnaround, and his diploma was the perfect symbol of his success .

Yet despite all of his immense success on the court, LeBron never let his stardom get to his head. His mother always made sure that her son had his priorities in order, and that meant having to focus on school first before basketball. This positive parental influence eventually did rub off on LeBron, as evident by the fact he once turned down an invitation to spend time with a former NBA player because it had been a school night. In a time where he needed the support most, when his doubts where spiraling out of control as to whether or not he should leave high school early, his mother and the rest of his support system were there to keep him grounded and

21

on the right track.

Despite all the naysayers doubting if LeBron would even graduate high school in the first place, he managed to prove every one of them wrong, including himself. By pulling through and graduating, he put a cap to one of the most storied high school careers of our generation, and the public now knew that LeBron James as not just a one-dimensional "basketball player" but a regular high school kid – one who had just made his mother the proudest parent in the world.

It was the perfect end to LeBron's high school career, and the perfect opportunity would pop up just in time for LeBron to fully grasp it following his graduation.

Stars Align

NBA Draft Lottery 2003. Russ Granik, the NBA's Deputy Commissioner at the time, was in charge of drawing the lottery for the NBA teams for that year's draft. Thousands of die-hard fans tuned in from all over the world to see if their team had a chance to obtain the best players coming out of college to bring glory to their respective teams. Scouts and NBA executives were just as eager, knowing full well that the draft could make or break their season for them – either bringing immense hope for their fans or just another year of disparity and loss.

The Cleveland Cavaliers were one of those teams who were all too familiar with the latter. Having not had any playoff breakthroughs since 1997, and with no definitive all-star to bring them hope of a better future, the Cavs and their fans were yearning for some sort of hero to save them from their distress.

Russ Granik had three letters in front of him, signifying the top three teams in that year's draft. With a clear voice, he loudly exclaimed, "The first pick in the 2003 NBA Draft goes to the Cleveland Cavaliers."

Thousands of Cavalier fans were beaming with excitement. Finally they had something worth celebrating and something to hope for. After the draft, many Cavalier fans turned their eyes away from the television, and towards the spotlight shining on LeBron James. It would be the perfect story - the local up and coming superstar from neighboring Akron fulfilling the role of the very hero who was going to save the Cavalier franchise. After all the speculation as to whether LeBron should have opted in for the draft the previous year, it seemed like the stars aligned for him. It seemed that he had been destined to finish high school and get his diploma.

Out of all the fans watching the draft lottery that night, LeBron was one of them. Suddenly all the talk of going to college had faded. Many college recruiters had been scouting LeBron for months, but now it seemed that he was on the cusp of something bigger and better. Now, he had a chance to not just become an NBA star – he was going to be a hometown hero.

A New Beginning

The reporter sat opposite Gloria and continued firing questions away regarding her prodigal son. LeBron's mother was used to this by now; her boy's talents and work ethic were ideal and prime for him to make history as one of the greatest basketball players to ever play the game, and she knew every reporter, fan and scout wanted to get to know as much as they could about LeBron as they followed his journey to superstardom.

Players with such gifted ability like LeBron only come around once in a lifetime. Everyone knew this, and wanted him to take the plunge and play on basketball's biggest stage as soon as possible – to see just how he would develop and match up against the very best in the world. Every reporter, friend and fan would subtly yet consistently seduce him to entertain that very idea. LeBron himself had fallen prey to it multiple times in his junior year, but after a rocky road and a lot of ups-and-downs, he had graduated high school and could now fully devote himself to the prospect of turning pro.

The early childhood dreams of bringing his family out of poverty and towards a better life suddenly did not seem all too far off. The world fixated their eyes on the high school phenom, finally ready to summit basketball's greatest mountain.

CHAPTER FIVE

NBA CAREER

"I treated it like every day was my last day with a basketball." – LeBron James

THE NBA. THE BIGGEST STAGE IN BASKETBALL, showcasing the brightest talents the world had yet to see. It was the perfect place for LeBron James to make his name - and for a future king to rise and make claim to the throne. All of his aspirations, all of his dreams, had built up and converged on this moment, and with a few more seconds away from his first NBA game, LeBron knew it was time to announce his presence to the league. His first opponent – the Sacramento Kings.

Only a couple of months before, LeBron had been selected first overall by his hometown team, the Cleveland Cavaliers, a move that surprised no one - causing massive excitement to not only Cavs fans but basketball fans all over the world. After all the drama, controversy and media hype that surrounded LeBron throughout his years in high school, he had finally made the leap to the big leagues, where high school status could only get you so far. Some people say the NBA stands for the "No Boys Allowed" league, and this young high school kid wanted to make sure that people didn't just view him as a schoolboy but a legitimate threat. The best way to do that was to show up when it mattered most, and the first taste of conquest for the King would be against Sacramento.

About nine minutes into the game, and the Cavs announcer encapsulated the excitement of the hometown crowd, shrieking, "Here he comes the other way... There's your first James jam!"

With lightning quick precision, LeBron stole the ball from his opponent, sprinted down the court and finished with an emphatic dunk to the uproar of the Cavs home fans as they erupted in delight at the arrival of their new superstar in the making. LeBron certainly didn't disappoint for the rest of the game: he put a wide array of skills on display, from passing to scoring, stealing and dunking, all to the delight of his home fans.

For all the hype that surrounded one of the most storied and media-covered players entering the league, the performance of LeBron James as a first year rookie, let alone one straight out of high school was even better than what most fans, critics and analysts expected of him.

His debut performance against the Sacramento

Kings had him at 25 points, an NBA record for most points scored by a prep-to-pro player in their respective debut. He finished his rookie year off with averages of 20.9 points, 5.5 rebounds and 5.9 assists per game, being only one of four players in NBA history to average such a stat line for their rookie season. To top it all off, he finished out his inaugural year with the coveted Rookie of the Year Award - once again to no one's surprise.

Fans were ecstatic to have a new superstar to celebrate. With tattoos on his body such as "Chosen One", "Witness" and "Gifted Child", LeBron obviously relished his natural prowess, and his performance on the court reflected that. Fans enjoyed witnessing a prodigy put on a show on the court, sending waves of awe throughout the stands and the entire league.

LeBron's debut season was nothing short of spectacular. As one of the only few players to go straight to the pros out of high school and succeed with such effortlessness, he made it all look so easy and smooth. However, the rest of his career would be anything but, as despite his personal heroics and accolades on the court, the Cavaliers were still a sinking ship. LeBron had breathed new hope and life into the franchise, letting them win 18 more games than they had their previous season, but they were still far from contenders amongst all the other teams in the league.

This would continue for several more seasons for LeBron. It was an undisputed fact that was the face of the Cavalier franchise, and he would be the one to bring them the glory of winning a championship - but as you will see throughout his career, this feat would not be as easy to achieve as his own personal flashes of brilliance on the court. It would be like junior year in high school all over again: the media pressure, the doubts and the critics all having crucial roles to play in LeBron's career. Most of all, the pressures to win a championship would enable him shine as one of the brightest talents the NBA has ever witnessed but also eventually transform him into one of the most hated NBA players to ever grace a league court.

CHAPTER SIX

THE KING

" Ever since I was a kid, I was always the winner."-
LeBron James

GAME 3, 2006 NBA PLAYOFFS. The Cleveland
Cavaliers were up against the Washington Wizards.
The Cavs had just reached a playoff berth thanks to a
determined LeBron James. Thanks to his status as as
one of the most formidable rising forces the league
had ever come across, LeBron had led the Cavs had
to the playoffs for the first time in nearly eight years;
his prowess and leadership had finally sparked a fire
within the Cavaliers that gave them the opportunity
to fight for an NBA title. At this stage in his career,
LeBron had slowly but surely built a reputation as the
man who put the Cavs' hopes and dreams on his own

shoulders as he carried them throughout hardships, trials and obstacles to get where they needed to go. It was overtime of Game 3, and it was time for LeBron to do that once more.

The Cavs were down 119 to 120 against the Wizards with only 3.6 seconds left on the clock. The

Cavs, its fans, as well as the Wizards knew exactly who was going to get the ball to save the day; it was just a matter of stopping him. When his people called on him to deliver when it mattered most, the King had to always deliver; this time, he would not disappoint.

"Hughes to play it in. Found James. LeBron.... To the hoop....FOR THE WIN.... HE GOT IT!!!!!" The Cavs announcer shrieked in excitement. Cavs fans were jumping out of their seats, the Wizards were frantically in a panic not knowing what to do, and LeBron simply backpedalled to defense for the final 0.9 seconds in the game. He didn't even have to play at this point - everyone in that building knew that the Cavs had won the game. It was all thanks to LeBron's last second heroics.

A King was officially born.

LeBron had driven baseline aggressively and laid the ball in to clinch the championships with a cold blooded game winner, shattering the Wizards' hopes and bringing the Cavs to glory. It was LeBron's first game winner, and it was a huge one. Just 2 games ago against the very same team he racked up a triple double in his playoff debut to stun the Wizards and clinch a victory for his Cavs. Now he would stun them again with his theatrical game winner.

With all the weight of the Cavs' world on his shoulders, LeBron proved up to the challenge. He assumed the burden of being the leader of his team, and as a leader, all his teammates followed suit. The responsibility to live up to this position each and every day was a tough, grueling job, but one perfectly suited for LeBron. This status of leader would be cemented by one definitive title – The King.

LeBron's meteoric rise now transcended that of just a sensational hero. He was a legitimate contender and superstar known widely across the entire league. He was breaking records all over the NBA and defining possibilities from what many thought to be impossible to achieve.

Year by year, in only a span of a couple of seasons, LeBron's performance and game would increase dramatically. His season-long averages would increase across all statistics, with his peak in points per game being at 31.4. Talks of MVP began to circulate across the league, as he finished 2nd in MVP voting in only his 4th NBA season, just behind Steve Nash. In these pivotal first few years where he earned his first playoff berth, LeBron had gotten a taste of what it was like playing on the biggest stage in basketball, and he was flourishing on all accounts.

The King had learned and become familiar with the lay of the land, it was now his time to conquer it.

The King's Conquest

Six seasons had passed since LeBron James had entered the league to roaring support and admiration. By the 2008-2009 seasons, he had amassed thousands of highlights, countless accolades, records, awards, All-Star Game MVPs and the undying support from his fans all over the world. His signature chase down block had become a fan-favorite, where he would sprint down the floor chasing an opponent who seemingly had an open lay-up or dunk only to swat the ball away at the very last moment, denying the opponent any chance of scoring. The King had begun his rule, and in the process had made NBA moments that would go down as some of the most legendary highlights in NBA history.

One of these moments was during Game 5 of the 2007 NBA Conference Finals. The Cavs were up against the Detroit Pistons. The Pistons were definitely a more formidable team, having more experienced players such as Chauncey Billups and Rasheed Wallace. The Pistons were no stranger to playoff victories either, having won the NBA Finals against the Lakers' dynamic duo of Shaq and Kobe back in 2004. They were heavily favored to win according to the fans and critics. However, it wasn't up to them - it was the players, with LeBron arguably the greatest of them all.

In Game 5, LeBron would put on an historical performance against the Pistons, scoring a total of 48 points, 29 of Cleveland's last 30 points, as well as the late game-winner – much to the chagrin of the completely stunned Pistons. Symbolic of the jersey number he had worn throughout his career at that point, his performance was undoubtedly "Jordan-esque", symbolic of how the greatest player of all time, Michael Jordan, would single-handedly take over games to lead his team to victory.

Chauncey Billups, the leader of the Pistons, sat down at the podium in disappointment, facing the swarm of reporters that were all just as stunned as he was. "We threw everything we had at him," Chauncey said begrudgingly. "We just couldn't stop him."

"We just couldn't stop him" – words fitting to describe LeBron's career leading up to that point. In just a couple of years the high school phenom had raised his status in NBA history with an almost effortless performance. Nobody was going to get in his way of whatever lands and lofty goals he set out to conquer – he simply could not be stopped.

At that point, it was only a matter of time before the highest honor for a basketball player made its way to LeBron - The MVP Award.

A Crown for a King

After 6 seasons, Lebron led his team to a 66-16 record (the best in the NBA that season) and averaged yet another remarkable stat line of 28.4 points, 7.6 rebounds, 7.2 assists, 1.7 steals, and 1.2 blocks per game. While the previous MVP awards eluded him due to his team not performing up to the standards of the league, this time no one had any reason to doubt – LeBron James was (and still is) the best player in the world. With the best record in the league as well as season averages that would put most NBA players to shame, he became the first Cavalier to win the MVP award.

Finally, the King had a crown to his name. He would go on to win three more MVPs with relative ease throughout his career.

At this point, you may think LeBron's rise to prominence was one of definite ease; the kid with unbelievable natural talents honing them to a point where he would be unmatched in superiority throughout the league. While that might have been true to a certain extent, every superstar goes through massive challenges and scrutiny on the road to greatness. The King had become satiated with his accolades at this point. All the goals he set out to conquer he had done so with relative ease, and it was now time to reach for the most valuable goal of them all. The King wanted a ring – a definitive throne for His Highness.

It would be in this journey that LeBron would face the most unbelievable pain, agony, scrutiny and eventual hatred that has ever surrounded any athlete in sports history. The road to the crown may have been relatively easy, but the road to the throne - and the ring - would be one faced with immense peril.

CHAPTER SEVEN

ROAD TO THE THRONE

" I won at every level – all the way since I started playing the game of basketball at nine. I've won at every level, won championships at every level. And, you know, it won't be fulfilled until I win at the highest level. "- LeBron James

UNLIKE ALL THE OTHER LANDS LeBron had conquered with relative ease, the quest for rings seemed particularly elusive. Nobody doubted LeBron's ability to absolutely reign terror on the court and dominate whichever opponent he chose to – but as the years passed and seasons went by, people started to doubt if LeBron could do what *really* mattered – win. No NBA legend has their legacy fully solidified until they had won an NBA championship. From old legends like Michael Jordan, Magic Johnson and Larry Bird to even newer ones like Kobe Bryant and Tim Duncan, all these players had something in common: they were all winners. LeBron had secured his legacy as a king, but to really join this elite group of players, he needed to have a ring.

LeBron had built his team up as a mainstay, top contending team in the Eastern Conference for several years, but every time they had made a push to the championship, they came up short. While a lot of these failures were attributed to growing pains in the first couple of years, LeBron was now a fully matured, fully realized superstar in the league and had every reason to win immediately. 2010 was his last contractual year in Cleveland, and if he wanted to win a championship for his hometown, he had to do it then.

2010 Eastern Conference Semi-Finals. The Cavs had once again clinched the best record in the entire NBA, and LeBron had won yet another MVP award. A couple of years ago, this was big news to LeBron and the Cavs – but LeBron's dominance had become so commonplace that this was expected of him by now, and year by year the best team record and the MVP awards consistently made their way to Cleveland. LeBron and the Cavs were targeting a different goal now – the coveted Larry O'Brien trophy.

They were to face the Boston Celtics, and after 5 grueling games battling back-and-forth, the Cavs found themselves down 3-2, fighting for their lives and a slim chance to stay in playoff contention. All their hard work all season long came down to that very game. The Cavs had always been arch-rivals with the Celtics, having being halted in their tracks year after year and never advancing to the Finals due to them. The Celtics were simply more experienced, with three future Hall-of-Famers in Paul Pierce, Ray Allen and Kevin Garnett making up the core of their team. Now with the future of the Cavs hanging in the balance, the team had called upon their King to carry them on to the Promised Land once again, the same way he had done for years – only this time, things would pan out differently.

It was the 4th Quarter, with about 1 minute and 20 seconds left to the game. The Celtics held a definitive 9-point lead on the Cavs, and had been leading throughout most of the game. The Celtics fans at the

TD Garden could smell blood, and were looking for the final kill to break the heart of LeBron and punch their own ticket on the way to the Conference Finals. LeBron was doing all he could to keep his team alive. Like a war general, he pulled out whatever weapons he had in his arsenal, shouted orders on the court and demanded only the best of his team. He so desperately wanted to keep his season alive, but his personal blunders got the better of him.

He drove to the right baseline and tried to pull his signature cross-court pass to the wide-open shooter in the corner.

"James... Lost it again! Unbelievable! His 9th turnover of the night!" The commentator was in utter disbelief at what he had witnessed from the King on the supposedly most important game of his. The Celtics were calmly dismantling the Cavs offense bit by bit, while LeBron was crumbling underneath the immense pressure his team had placed upon him. The Cavs tried to heave one more desperate 3 point attempt to cut into the lead, but the ball rolled in and out of the rim – almost mocking and taunting the King's apparent failure to his city of Cleveland.

The Cavs had lost – not only their chance of winning an NBA title (the year where every fan, analyst and player had expected them to), but their superstar in LeBron James. LeBron's contract was ending that very year, and everyone knew that if the Cavs had fallen short of an NBA championship once again, the possibility of their King leaving his home were going to skyrocket. Cleveland could only hold their breath and hope for the best – that their King would choose to stay in his hometown.

Legacy and Loyalty Questioned

It was a bitter end to the King's season in Cleveland, as once again, the ring eluded him. His legacy seemed to be in the balance once more. Whether or not LeBron was going to abandon Cleveland, as well as the hopes and dreams of his fans, was entirely up to him. As he finished shaking the hands of the entire Celtics team, LeBron grimaced and walked off the court and into the tunnels. His face was stricken with disappointment. He looked down as if all hope were lost for him in Cleveland. He was faced with an impossible decision – stay loyal to his hometown even though he had not won a championship for close to 8 years, or leave Cleveland in pursuit of conquering his goals in different lands.

Only LeBron knew what he was going to do, and as he took off his jersey, many Cavs fans wondered if that was the last time LeBron was going to wear the colors of a Cleveland Cavalier.

It was LeBron's decision to make, and nobody at that moment knew just how this very "decision" would completely alter the landscape of the NBA for years to come.

CHAPTER EIGHT
THE DECISION

"Maybe my pain was my motivation." – LeBron James

JULY 8 2010 – The city of Cleveland was shaken in a way it had ever experienced. From afar, it would have seemed that the city was gripped by complete chaos and rioting – and to a certain extent, it was. Flames started to fill the streets as cries of "traitor" started to echo throughout the city.

On the other side of the country however, the city of Miami was experiencing a joy unlike any other. In complete stark contrast to the events occurring in Cleveland, fireworks started to fill the skies, posters started to rise, and billboards were erected. Throughout the city, cries of celebration and tears of joy were seen in turn.

The impetus for this drama had been an announcement - just six simple words spoken by LeBron James. The results were the world undergoing a frenzy unlike any other. With his big decision to leave Cleaveland for Miami, the man that was once deemed "The King" had now fallen from grace, and was insulted as "The Traitor" or "The Quitter".

The Cavaliers team owner, Dan Gilbert, was incensed. He issued an open letter to the fans of the Cavs: "I PERSONALLY GUARANTEE THAT THE CLEVELAND CAVALIERS WILL WIN AN NBA

CHAMPIONSHIP BEFORE THE SELF-TITLED FORMER 'KING' WINS ONE."

His anger echoed the sentiments shared by millions of heartbroken Cleveland fans around the nation. Only moments before Gilbert's vitriolic rage, LeBron had hosted a live television special, aptly named "The Decision", to announce which team he would join now that he was a free agent. After his heart-breaking loss and disappointing season-ending failure to what was supposed to be a championship winning year for him, speculations as to where LeBron might end up were spreading like wildfire. On July 8th, those questions were answered.

LeBron sat across from the reporter with a calm, yet anxious look. Finally, a couple of minutes into the program, the big question was asked: "The answer to the question everybody wants to know - LeBron, what's your decision?"

The nerves in the room - and of everyone watching from home that night – were at their peak. With a poker face, LeBron spoke the words that would cause an uproar of immense proportions throughout basketball's landscape: "I'm going to **take**

my talents to South Beach, and join the Miami Heat." These six words were all it took – "take my talents to South Beach" – and in an instant, the world of the NBA changed, seemingly forever.

The King, the hometown hero, was leaving his city. Many felt betrayed by LeBron's decision, as the life that he had breathed into his city seven years ago was now all but gone. Everyone knew Cleveland was going to suffocate in his absence. The King was moving on, and the hope of building his empire in his hometown had dissipated just as he set his sights on new lands to establish his kingdom.

The Big Three

In Miami, LeBron would not be alone in pursuing his ever-elusive rings. He teamed up with perennial all-stars Dwyane Wade and Chris Bosh, effectively forming the first modern 'Big Three' of basketball. The Miami Heat had gone from a team struggling to barely reach the playoffs to an overpowered beast, which many analysts predicted would fly through the league to the Finals with relative ease. This was the primary motivation behind LeBron's decision – he wanted to win so badly and was willing to risk it all, even his reputation and hometown status, to do so. He was fully aware that whether or not he won or lost in Miami, would make or break his legacy as either one of the all-time celebrated greats or one of the most despised NBA players of all time. LeBron had always faced immense scrutiny throughout his playing years, but with his "Decision", the scrutiny and pressure to win increased by exponentially. Whether LeBron would retire a true King or a disappointment was hanging in the balance, and he now had no excuse not to deliver.

The Miami Heat had officially placed targets on their backs. With three of the top players in the entire league joining forces to dominate the NBA landscape, they had officially become the team to beat. With LeBron's overall dominance, mixed with Dwyane's quickness and Bosh's versatility, the Miami Heat cruised their way to the top of the league's rankings, and in the process became the most hated team in the entire NBA landscape.

Crowds of opposing fans would welcome them to their arena with boos and jeers, but Miami would still walk away with definitive victories, almost in an arrogant fashion. LeBron's reputation had taken a 180 degree turn from his first seven years in Cleveland. He had been used to the attention and scrutiny that surrounded him since high school, but never hatred by the general public to this extent. It was evident that his decision cost him millions of fans, and he did not know how to regain them. As a result, there was only one thing he could do – embrace it.

CHAPTER NINE

FROM KING TO TYRANT

"I like criticisms, it makes you strong."- LeBron James

FOR HIS ENTIRE FIRST YEAR IN MIAMI, LeBron relished in playing the villain's role. Stealing victories and breaking opposing fans' hearts had become what he was known for, and he did so with such a brazen and nonchalant attitude which further amplified his status as the villain of the league. His status as the King had now evolved – he was The Tyrant, a proud, cocky, arrogant beast who could not be beat, and who everyone loved to hate. Whoever dared to challenge him would be stopped dead in their tracks mercilessly.

LeBron and the Heat carried this attitude of theirs

all the way to the NBA Finals. Now affectionately dubbed "The Heatles" (with respect to the band, The Beatles) by their own fans, The Heat were to face an old nemesis in the Dallas Mavericks. The Heat's players were young, athletic, cocky and confident – rightfully so considering how they managed to reach so far into the playoffs with such relative ease. The Mavericks on the other hand, were a little old, a little rusty, and a little slow but still with a lot of experience on their side – and they were being led by veterans Dirk Nowitzki and Jason Kidd. The Heat had faced the Mavericks back in the 2006 Finals. Things were different then, with the Mavericks being the favorite to win it all, only to be upset by a personal "Jordan-esque" performance by Dwyane Wade, who had single-handedly carried his team over the Mavericks to win the title. It had been five years since, and both Miami and Dallas were looking to reclaim a chance at victory once more. It was only fitting that they faced each other once again. With so much hype and story from their previous bout, it was a rematch for the ages.

This time, however, the Heat was the heavily-favored ones to win. They had everything Dallas did not, and everyone expected the Heat to overpower

Dallas the same way they had been overpowering every other team in the league the past year. It was a David versus Goliath battle - the Heat being the ferocious giant of a monster, while the Mavericks being the noble yet confident underdogs. However, staying true to the story, Dallas would pull one of the most storied comebacks and victories ever witnessed in an NBA Finals game.

Game 2, 2011 NBA Finals. After a decisive victory for Miami in Game 1 of the NBA Finals, everything had fallen true to people's expectations. The Heat were out-jumping, out-hustling and simply out-playing the entire Mavericks team, and by the middle of the 4th quarter of Game 2, the Heat held a 15 point lead. However, what seemed like another definitive victory by the Heat would be far from it. The series of events that were to unfold in the following six minutes of play would be forever etched in the minds of Heat fans all over the world.

"Terry's wide open, and gets it to go." Jason Terry calmly knocked down a baseline jumper. The announcer showed no signs of excitement or enthusiasm for whatever the Mavericks were doing at this point – everyone thought the game was a done deal. "Kidd throws it ahead to Terry, and...Terry the layup." The Mavericks scored 2 quick buckets to cut the lead to 11, and prompted the Heat to take a quick timeout. The Heatles were still relatively calm, not thinking much of the quick run the Mavericks seemed to be putting on. Little did they know how much this would change in a matter of minutes.

Fast forward a couple of more minutes into the game, and things had taken a turn for the worse for the Heat. The Heat announcer, with a breath of excitement in his speech that was previously non-existent, suddenly seemed all too interested in the game. "Nowitzki... puts it up.... PUTS IT IN! 2 POINT

GAME!" Everyone in the stadium started to sweat from worry. The Mavs had fought all the way back from a 15 point deficit to cut it to just 2 points, and suddenly all the attention had gone to LeBron to once again carry his team over the hump. However, the once great and omnipresent LeBron was nowhere to be found. Dirk simply took advantage and stole the show.

"Nowitzki...drives...underneath lefty lay up BANKS IT IN!!" Dirk had just scored a beautiful left-handed lay up to give his team the lead after overcoming a huge deficit in the 4th quarter. The announcer was the only one shouting with excitement, filling the silence that had engulfed the entire Heat arena. Dirk Nowitzki and his Mavs had sent a bold statement to the Heat; they were not going to simply relent like how all the other teams in the playoffs had. With that stunning victory and beautiful display of basketball Nowitzki put on, the entire basketball world was suddenly a Dallas Mavericks fan. Nobody thought that the Heat could be beaten, but now that one team had showed the world the impossible, everyone put their hopes in the Mavs as the "heroes" destined to defeat the "villains" of the league.

LeBron and the Heat were faced with an unfamiliar situation. Not having lost a home game in the playoffs yet, the Heat were stunned and confused, and suddenly doubts begin to creep into the players' mind as to whether they were able to win the NBA title.

Casting doubts was all the Mavericks had to do, because once there was a chink exposed in the Heat's supposedly formidable armor, their attack was relentless. Heat fans were watching with disappointment, while everyone else rejoiced in witnessing the downfall they had always wanted to see. Everybody looked to LeBron to see just where and how he would lead his team to victory. Like all the other greats that came before him when faced with adversity, it was the MVP, the leader of the team that would lead them over the hump, willing their respective teams to victory. With all the hype that surrounded LeBron throughout his entire career - his tattoos, his status as "The Chosen One" and "The King" - he had failed to deliver in a spectacular fashion. "The Chosen One" had become "The Frozen One", freezing up and shrinking under basketball's greatest spotlight.

As a result, the Mavericks stole a championship away from the Heat, denying LeBron yet again of another chance to win an NBA title. One look at his stat sheet throughout the entire series and you would be surprised that LeBron was the same tyrannical beast that everyone had feared. His 4th quarter performance was disheartening, and where people expected him to exert his will onto the team, he did just the opposite, averaging a measly 17.8 points per game in the Finals, and at one point even scoring just 8 points an entire game. The world was delighted; LeBron was devastated. The Tyrant had officially fallen off his high horse, and even with a stellar group of teammates around him, the ring once more was not his to win. He had risked everything to get an NBA title, and it seemed like he had failed, losing everything in the process.

The King that everybody once loved, now the Tyrant that everybody loved to hate, had just solidifed his status as a loser on the greatest stage of basketball. If there was any thing left to salvage from his career reputation before the Finals, it would have been his honor in delivering what his team desperately asked of him – but even that now had faded into obscurity.

Lebron risked everything to win, and even when he had no excuses not to, he still had failed in extravagant fashion.

CHAPTER TEN

ROAD TO REDEMPTION

"Don't be afraid of failure. This is the way to

succeed." – Lebron James

AT THIS POINT, THE WORLD WAS CELEBRATING LEBRON'S FAILURE and counting him out. Nobody believed in him anymore. The once great "King" had diminished into the most hated player in the enitre league - one who simply could not win a title and cement his legacy as an all-time great. The scrutiny, media pressure and hatred surrounding LeBron was at its peak, and when no one seemed to believe in him, he had to believe in himself. For someone who had gone through and achieved so much in his NBA career already, he was still in his prime, and only in his twenties. He knew he had a lot more to give, and the shot of reaching basketball immortality was still possible.

The role of villain had suited him for one whole season, but it was not serving him any longer. He relinquished his role as the Tyrant of the NBA, and refocused all of his energy into one singular goal – to win a championship. No more fun, no more games, and no more antics on or off the court. He knew that if he came up short once again, his legacy would be forever tainted as "The King Without a Ring". This coming of age and maturation for LeBron was pivotal for his redemption. He began to humble himself. He no longer shunned the fans, critics and general public. He began to open up, and in return some of the world was ready to reciprocate. LeBron knew if he didn't win a title the next season, the title of "The King" would officially be dead, his legacy forever remembered as one of a disappointment. It was now or never for LeBron, and he chose now.

The next season, the Heat once again found themselves cruising throughout the league, defeating teams with relative ease. The crazy media attention and villainous potrayal of the Heat had quietened down with respect to the previous season, partly due to LeBron's new approach and people simply getting used to the "Heatles" by then. Despite their unsurprising success in the regular season, it was the playoffs that mattered most to the Heat. Anything short of a championship would be deemed a failure – everyone in the Heat locker room knew this – and ever since last year's debacle at the Finals, they were more than ready to get another shot.

In order for LeBron to finally get over the hump, he had to face his old demons and conquer them once and for all. Fittingly, one of these demons would come in the form of an old nemesis that had once brutally denied him from reaching basketball's highest peak sparked the series of events that led to his "decision," tyranny and eventual downfall at the Finals. Lebron's story was about to come full circle.

Old Demons

2 seasons ago, LeBron James and the Cavs were supposed to win an NBA title, but were harshly halted by the Boston Celtics, which ultimately led him to leaving Cleveland to join forces with the Miami Heat. Many had speculated that if LeBron were to have won that series against the Celtics, he would have won a championship, stayed in Cleveland and avoided the entire following mess that had ensued. Nobody knew

if LeBron could have actually won, but during the 2012 Eastern Conference Finals, they were about to get their answer.

The Miami Heat was now matched up against the Boston Celtics - the exact same Celtics who had caused a whirlwind in the entire city of Cleveland. Two seasons had passed since that fateful game, and now people were wondering if their former King had matured enough to take on his old rivals and finally beat them. Had LeBron really developed enough as a player and a champion that could help his team when it mattered most? Did he make the right decision to leave Cleveland and join the Heat? There was no other story set up so perfectly – LeBron had one more shot at facing his old demons. The only question that remained was if he was finally going to conquer them.

Game 6, 2012 Eastern Conference Finals.

What would unfold as a comeback by the Heat started off with critics, fans and the world counting them out once again. LeBron was in a familiar situation. Battling the old yet still gritty Celtics for 5 games, LeBron once again found himself down 3-2. With an impending Game 6, the future of Lebron's season was on the line. However, this time it represented so much more than just a 'Win or Go Home' game. **If Lebron were to lose this game, his career would've been done for for good.** No amount of redemption could possibly justify losing to the Celtics twice and coming short of a title two years in a row - especially with the overpowered weapons LeBron had with the Heat. If he lost this game, more than just the season would be over for him; his entire career, legacy, reputation and honor would have no chance of ever resurfacing. Of all the scrutiny LeBron faced throughout his years of playing, none was more intense than that very Game 6 looming over him. The pressure of carrying the load of an overhyped, overpowered Heat - one that promised their fans that they were going to win multiple championships – rested on none other than LeBron's broad shoulders. Those shoulders had carried this responsibility multiple times throughout his career, but the weight of that Game 6 was unlike any other load he had had to burden himself with before.

Everything was at stake for him. It was "Win or Go Home", but more importantly, it was "Win, or Be Forever Humiliated as the Laughingstock of the NBA".

Either way, LeBron had to win and face his demons once and for all. This time, he would conquer them in an inhuman and otherworldly display of dominance – almost as if he was a man possessed by demons of his own.

CHAPTER ELEVEN

A MAN POSSESSED

"I think team first. It allows me to succeed, it allows my team to succeed."- LeBron James

"I'M NOT SURE IF I'VE EVER SEEN LeBron James like that. Not even when he scored 45 against Detroit. On that night, he looked like a man possessed." ESPN analyst Stephen A. Smith is known for his often loud and hysterical sporting rants on television, but this time he had nothing but praise and admiration for the King. "This performance is one of the all-time greatest performances in playoff history, right up next to MJ's 63 against Boston."

With everything on the line, LeBron James had no choice but to deliver. His usual fun and playful demeanor on the court had transformed into a serious scowl of ferocity. He did not smile, he did not interact with anyone in the arena, and he showed no emotion. He was all business from the moment he stepped into the building. This do-or-die killer mentality led him to have one of the greatest moments in NBA playoffs history.

TD Garden was absolutely electric and abuzz, waiting to spur on their Celtics to one more win closer to advancing to the NBA Finals. The Boston fans were familiar with LeBron, and had become a fan-favourite of taunts, mockery and insults even back when he was a Cavalier. Now with everything on the line the jeers had only amplified, as they could not wait to steal a victory from LeBron once again - or so they thought.

It was midway through the first half, and things had already not gone according to plan for the Celtics fans. The announcer summed up the entire situation succinctly: "Is it possible that he's had a quiet 24 points? Maybe because it's quiet in the building."

What was once a loud and gregarious crowd all waiting to usher LeBron's career down the drain had turned silent. LeBron had put on a show, single-handedly scoring close to half of his team's points, and having an answer for every punch the Celtics tried to throw at him. A player that tried to guard him was like a sheep getting ready to be sent for slaughter. It was a massacre - a complete demolition of Celtic pride and the old demons that LeBron had so struggled to conquer in the past.

Similar to his previous historic game against Detroit, LeBron was simply unstoppable – hell bent on making sure his legacy stayed intact and that his kingdom did not suffer anymore losses than it already had. Yet unlike the game against Detroit, this time LeBron destroyed his opponent with an emotionless stone-cold ferocity – leaving the entire arena shivering as the tempeature dropped each time LeBron made a difficult shot or overtly exerted his dominance on the court. It was only the first half, but LeBron's unbelievable performance had already drained the spirits out of TD Garden.

Chris Bosh had the ball, executed a post spin move and attempted to score a left handed hook shot above the outstretched arm of his defender. The ball clanked on the side of the rim, but out of nowhere the announcer broke the silence: "OH JAMES COMES FLYING IN... AND THROWS IT DOWN!"

LeBron exploded above every other Celtic defender. In a monstrous symbol of dominance, he threw a massive putback dunk to the dismay of Celtics fans - a fitting play which summed up the rest of the game. It didn't matter what his teammates did that night, whether or not they missed or made shots. This time, when the King's number was called, he was sure as hell going to make sure he answered it, and that no one was going to get in his way.

All the lights, hype and media attention faded from Lebron's viewpoint. They did not matter anymore. The one thing that did matter was the last chance to save whatever was left of his career and his legacy. This consumed him, ate at him each and every possession – slowly gnawing away at his psyche until he simply could not take losing anymore. He had lost so much; he was not going to lose the one chance he had left in making his career and choices right. He had evolved, and become completely detached from his own mind and the eyes of everyone looking at him. LeBron James had transcended from bothbeing the cocky kid from Ohio and the arrogant villain in Miami.

He was indeed a man possessed.

The Coronation

Lebron scored 30 points in the first half alone, and finished the game with an unbelievable stat line of 45 points, 15 rebounds and 5 assists – statistics only eclipsed by one other player in NBA history, Wilt Chamberlain. That Game 6 was by far the most important game in LeBron James' playing career, and after 2 seasons of shrinking under the pressure he finally showed up, matured and ready to conquer his past demons once and for all. The Heat went on to beat the Celtics in Game 7 and ultimately won the Finals with relative ease against the young Oklahoma City Thunder.

"The King without a Ring" would no longer ring true to LeBron's status. After nine long, painful and arduous seasons, he finally hoisted the Larry O'Brien Trophy in front of his adoring Heat fans. For once, everyone that had shunned him had nothing to criticize anymore. He had done what he set out to do, and the risks he had taken to get his championship finally paid off. It took maturity, growth and a lot of development from LeBron to finally conquer his demons and humble himself enough to win the championship.

As Dorris Burke went to the podium to interview LeBron after winning it all, nobody could disagree with the first words that came out of LeBron's mouth: "It's about damn time."

CHAPTER TWELVE

LONG LIVE THE KING

"I don't need too much. Glamor and all that stuff don't excite me. I am just glad I have the game of basketball in my life." – LeBron James

LEBRON'S REIGN WOULD CONTINUE for one more season with the Heat, bringing them to the Finals once more, and clinching another championship - this time against the San Antonio Spurs. With two Finals MVP Awards, back-to-back championships, and multiple MVP awards, Lebron's legacy at this point was firmly intact regardless of whether the fans loved him or hated him,.

The Championships were definite coronations for The King. Now with a completely new mature and positive demeanour, LeBron had a certain calmness about him. It finally seemed that all the years of scrutiny and agony had molded him into not only a better basketball player but a better man. Still fun-loving and gregarious off the court, LeBron made up for it in his seriousness towards his work ethic on the court, and the dominance he still continues to display each and every day.

With old superstars like Kobe Bryant and Tim Duncan about to hang up their jerseys for good, everyone knows that LeBron is primed to take full control of the league and relish in his position as the true King. No more tyrannical antics for LeBron anymore. As the global icon for the game of basketball he knows he has a tough burden to carry on his shoulders, but considering everything that he has been through in his life to this point, carrying responsibilities and burdens should no longer be a problem for him.

LeBron's story will go down as one of the most

colorful and historic of our time. Traveling a true hero's journey for the man from Akron, Ohio, LeBron has tasted the bitterness of defeat, the agony of ordeals, but also the spoils of victory. Only a King would be able to survive such intense tribulations in his reign, and as a result LeBron is now able to live up to that name to its fullest degree.

CHAPTER THIRTEEN

RETURN OF THE KING

"I'm LeBron James from Akron, Ohio ... From the inner

city ... I'm not even supposed to be here.

I ain't got no worries." – Lebron James

THE KID FROM AKRON, OHIO had set out to win a championship, to redeem his city of Cleveland and bring them to the Promised Land. That had been the plan, but life had taken an unexpected turn for him. Now, about a decade into his NBA career, LeBron was a 2-time NBA Champion, multiple MVP award winner and overall league superstar. Although his reputation had taken a hit by "taking his talents to South Beach", the adoration and admiration that came from winning NBA titles had softened some the hate he had received and helped him reclaim some of the love he had lost since his infamous decision. Yet the bitter aftertaste of him leaving Cleveland was still present and strong for many fans. There would be no better redemption arc for the hometown hero than to return to his home with the elixir he had earned from his journeys on the road, and after 4 NBA seasons away from his hometown, with many lessons learned in the process, LeBron James stunned the world with yet another "decision".

Ready to bring the skills and lessons he acquired by summiting basketball's highest mountain back to Cleveland, LeBron James was coming home.

With all the history between LeBron and Cleveland, a storied past would be an understatement to LeBron's legacy with the Cavs and his hometown. From celebrated to hated and now embraced once more, LeBron has seen the best and worst of Cleveland, and just like any other relationship, stronger bonds can only be forged once having experienced both ends of that spectrum. With new promises and goals in mind, he definitely has not forgotten the vow to his hometown of bringing them the glory of a championship.

Armed with new knowledge of the game, championship experience and a better supporting cast around him in his team, the Cavs would win 53 games in the 2015 NBA season and punch their ticket to the Finals, making LeBron the first player to appear in 5 consecutive NBA Finals. The Cavs would eventually lose to a surging Warriors, but LeBron showcased his level of maturity, leadership and dominance in carrying his team to win 2 games without two of his key teammates in Kyrie Irving and Kevin Love, finishing with astounding averages of 35.8 points, 13.3 rebounds and 8.8 assists per game.

While LeBron has gone through more than any other player has ever had to go through in their NBA career (he has already played more minutes than NBA legends Magic Johnson and Larry Bird), he is still only 31 years of age, with lots of years left in his legs. Despite the rise of up and coming superstars like Stephen Curry and Kevin Durant, LeBron is still undoubtedly heralded as the best player in the world as of this moment. His impact is far-reaching and extends way beyond basketball, making him one of the most influential figures and athletes of our time.

With all the scrutiny and pressure LeBron has faced throughout his life, we can only marvel as we witness

"The Chosen One" grow up and mature his game before our very eyes. A player like LeBron only comes around once in a lifetime, and with record-breaking highlights and accolades at such a young age, who knows what else he has in store for us?

We can only sit back and relish the time "The King" has left on his throne. The legacy continues.

All hail the King.

Acknowledgments

Photo credits go to Keith Allison.
https://www.flickr.com/photos/keithallison/

Thanks for reading! Please add a short review on Amazon and let me know what you thought!

JOHN EMERSON

Printed in Great Britain
by Amazon